W0082106

HOW MANY FACES DO YOU HAVE?

Mike Schneider

Texas Review Press
Huntsville, Texas

Copyright @ 2017 by Mike Schneider
All rights reserved
Printed in the United States of America

FIRST EDITION

Requests for permission to acknowledge material from the work should be sent to:

Permissions
Texas Review Press
English Department
Sam Houston State University
Huntsville, TX 77341-2146

ACKNOWLEDGEMENTS:

The author thanks the editors of these publications where some of these poems, some in earlier versions & different titles, first appeared: The Way Your Fingers, *2001 Emily Dickinson Award Anthology* (West Universities Press, 2002); Hound Dog Blues, *Main Street Rag*, Fall 2009; Rainy November Again, *Motif 2: Chance*, Summer 2010; Buenos Aires, *Cimarron Review*, Winter 2011; The Trouble with Love, *U.S. 1 Worksheets*, vol. 57 (Princeton, NJ: 2012); Skin, *The Florida Review*, 37.2 (Winter 2012); Flight to Yucatan, *The Florida Review*, 37.2 (Winter 2012); River Under Ice, *U.S. 1 Worksheets*, vol. 59 (Princeton, NJ: 2014); Love Me Like the First Word, *Atlanta Review*, XXI no. 1 (Fall/Winter 2014); Mae West as an Apartment, *U.S. 1 Worksheets*, vol. 60, (Princeton, NJ: 2015); Song of the Old Shoes (Song of the Bruised Grapefruit), *Slipstream #35*, Summer 2015; I Want You, *The Comstock Review*, 29:1 (Spring/Summer 2015); Undercover, *U.S. 1 Worksheets*, vol. 61 (Princeton, NJ: 2016); Fou d'Asie, Montreal, *The New Guard*, vol. V (2016); About Time, *passager*, Summer 2016 (Honorable Mention, 2016 Poetry Contest); He Dreams a Woman Who's a Ship, *The Comstock Review*, 30:1 (Summer 2016).

Cover art: *Ceremonie*, 1998, (acrylic on canvas, 15.5" x 30"), by Maxon Jean-Louis, author's collection, from Galerie Macondo, Pittsburgh, Pa., www.artshaitian.com

Cover design: Nancy Parsons

Library of Congress Cataloging-in-Publication Data

Names: Schneider, Mike, 1946- author.

Title: How many faces do you have? : poetry / by Mike Schneider.

Description: First edition. | Huntsville, Texas : Texas Review Press, [2017]

Identifiers: LCCN 2017009815 (print) | LCCN 2017011188 (ebook) | ISBN 9781680031324 (pbk.) | ISBN 9781680031348 (ebook)

Subjects: LCSH: Intimacy (Psychology)--Poetry.

Classification: LCC PS3619.C4469 A6 2017 (print) | LCC PS3619.C4469 (ebook) | DDC 811/.6--dc23

LC record available at https://lccn.loc.gov/2017009815

With gratitude to family, teachers, friends & many poets.
Particular thanks to our Pittsburgh group of East End Poets.
And to Tony Hoagland & Jeff Worley.
Love to Ellie always.
Deep affection & joy in knowing Jan, her music.

Contents:

HOW MANY FACES DO YOU HAVE?

In the healing of that wound, which never closes,
lies the invented, strange qualities of a man's work.

—Lorca

Maybe God tried to turn you into a dumpster
so you could be lifted by the truck's hydraulic
arm and banged empty.

—Dean Young

About Time

for J. S. (1946-2009)

Accordion bleachers rolled back flat
to the wall along which nervous boys

clustered & postured to hide how much
we didn't know, ceiling lights dimmed

to moonglow. When the HiFi spun
Vinton's velvet tenor, it was the moment

to muster inner stuff. Like torn edges
of continents rejoined, you & I fit

each other. As time surged & unfolded
we oozed across the gym floor. We moved

& didn't. Your dress was blue & shiny.
I think it was made of glue. Your soft

places said *Welcome*. Rush of sunrise
inside me, *What's happening?* I wondered.

Your eyes, also blue, deeper than I had
world to know, said *Dreamer*. I faltered.

You tugged me closer, shore to lapping
sea, breath at my ear, a voice: *About time*

you learned to slow dance. Why does
music end? I was never more endlessly

seventeen. Words that love to play
hide & seek come in too late to tell you.

Skin

Suddenly awake, I shake
     my head & fold my arms to hold
myself. To feel myself
       breathing calms me

like the ocean calms intelligence—
       breath across the tongue, taste
of absence, words not there
       to say when she turned

& touched my arm. Two gypsies
       spiraling round a fire, two galaxies
drawn to the other's gravity,
       stretched & pulled away

from ourselves. I thought
       of sweltering summer, small
town, a boy & his three-legged
       dog named Eddie, how

he wobbled, Eddie, hot cinders
       on the sidewalk by the barber
shop, striped pole like a candy
       cane twirling slowly. Why

did I feel suddenly lonely
       as a stone? *Anything can happen,*
because nothing says it can't.
    She said that. *Let's have a collision*

that obliterates the silence
       of all the words ever spoken.
I heard myself say that. Christ,
    emptiness, nameless, where am I now?

Mae West as an Apartment

after Dalí, 1934-35

Why don't you drop by sometime?
she says, plumping the cushions of her
        lips as if they were a pink sofa
on which you might get lucky, maybe
    someday in one of your most wildass
dreams, if you don't think about it
    too much. From the left-open back door
of her mind, her eyes walk in like Goya
    & Velasquez, two old masters, two kinds
of disaster. They absorb you, unblinking
    & seem to declare: *Don't forget
to adore me, the cascade of my silver
    tresses like a tapestry
            invoking unsayable stories
        of what we do for love.*

You enter the space she makes
                & her face becomes a clock
on the mantel of her mother-bone
    shoulders, tick-tock, tick-
tock, as if she has by herself inadvertently
        invented time. *It's what*

*we have so everything doesn't happen
    at once,* she winks & whispers *Einstein
told me that.* When you learn to wait
                & forget to hope, only then
she may in your dream of a butterfly
    that dreams you emerge, whirled up
from the core of molten matter, a rose
        unfolding, centerpiece of all interior
design. *Hi, big boy,* she says, shifting
    her hips as she looks you over.

Flight to Yucatan

"Happiness is an angel with a grave face."
—Modigliani

Christmas morning, roaring
            south over rumpled hills
of cloud toward Playa del Carmen,
                  omelettes & apple pancakes
lofting through the cabin, zinfandel
                  to lift my wings, buoyantly
I'm noticing our flight attendant, waves
            of hair, sable touched with scarlet,
lustrous skin, a pin that says Tamara,
            her smile that says
      you're not the first to look at me.

Wordlessly I wish her happiness
            as down the aisle she brings
the warm container
            of herself. Tamara—
nice name, I tell her, thinking
            of the Goth queen in Shakespeare
who lived only for revenge.

Some people call me Tammy,
   she says with lips glossed persimmon.
We're just having fun here, I say
   to myself, and as she turns away want
to untie her apron, want to say
   I'm drowning in your brown eyes, your
dried-blood nails almost make me cry.

Beside me, flipping
        shiny pages
of an airline magazine, my wife
       lifts her eyes—umm, tasty
she says, taking a small bite
         of her apple pancake
with syrup. She smiles
       with icy sweetness, woman
I love, my life. Out the window,

stratospheric blue, thin skin
         of the planet, clouds
miles below, endless as belief
        & failed promises, vapor
that doesn't catch us when we fall
         through sky that shimmers
like a gift: July for Christmas. A face

is such a strange thing. Obsessed
        with distortion, Modigliani
loved elongated faces
   like Tamara's at a distance,
a flattened oval, two black jewels. He
       painted with a dagger
in his teeth, they say, to see the face
    within the face—grave,
cold-eyed as Nefertiti, Queen of Egypt,
     whom I've always loved
         for her name alone.

Song of the Old Shoes

with a line from Ginsberg

With your eyes of no money, tongue
like a match, strike anywhere, face
like the moon streaked with cloud
blown back like a stallion's black
hair, you occupy the city
    of my mind. Squadrons of you
patrol the streets, alleys
& backyards. I hide like a spy
under the floorboards. And in the attic
under the eaves where I hear rain.
I climb an apple tree to disappear
into the sky as if I were written
in invisible ink. The wind
blows through me & I read myself.
I'm still here. Children with their precious
backpacks walk to school. A crossing guard
says, *Be careful in this fog, you might get lost.*

*

November arrives with frosty
air. Across the moon's
penumbra, crows row upstream
in black canoes. They cry
& shake their fists at the umpire.
The tall grass is ochre & leans back
like Bacall blowing smoke.
You showed me how to be cruel
you say. Your words simmer out
        like a mist of fleas. They
get under my skin. They know
how to bite. I must have hurt you terribly
            in your last life.

*

We're an old pair of shoes.
We forget to get up for school.
Like backyard squirrels, tails
curled like questions, tiny paws
with an acorn held in prayer, teeth
that flash sharply as a well timed
compliment, we play at being
free. Whatever comes let it
come, we say, whatever spins
spins into the vortex
of our innocence, where sky dips
into the sea. And clouds are a feathery
chorus-line of dancers, one of whom,
spreading her legs, wants
to accept my small offering.
    I'm sick of all your sadness,
you say & I reply, *Oh grandmother
moonlight, the yellow gourd grows large
in the front garden. Sorrow is what we are.
Please send help. Send it via Western
Union. Tiger, tiger burning bright. Stop.*

Rainy November Again

Morning after the breakup, taste
of last night's coffee, love—
the mixmaster blender, grinder
setting—how it splatters
                you like cranberries
bleeding down the kitchen wall
because you forgot to hold the lid on
tight. It was Thanksgiving in Houston
            the year the hurricane
ripped through my brother's suburb
howling like some wounded animal
they haven't named yet. Days
that disappeared in shattered glass
from tall buildings. Lifetimes
                you spend to get it right
& never do. Chrysanthemums
for Nancy, my neighbor, thanks
for taking in my mail, and her husband
                    wants to stone me.
No good deed goes unpunished
says Jeffers, who likes to say things
            like that. Everything is change,
says Myles, who reads the Dalai Lama
& paints in late light, landscapes
like contusions with a purpled inner glow.

Hound Dog Blues

People all over the planet, millions of them,
are considerably more dead than I am,

I keep telling myself, and this woman
who fell asleep on my couch while I played

You Ain't Goin' Nowhere & other lonesome
songs on my best guitar is not to blame. Please,

she said, play, so I did. And my confidence,
already worn to a thin pale stone, is now lost

& hiding in the dark with hairy animals
who live underground & huddle close

at 55 degrees Fahrenheit, temperature of bones
in coffins. And it came up somehow, before

tired & becalmed she drifted, how Ginsberg
one afternoon, content after masturbating,

heard the voice of Blake & it sank within
to become his own prophetic rumble

from the Earth, like stones if they could speak
with rhythm & radiance. Like the rattling

I heard moments ago—a necklace
her daughter made, small stones scattered

on my hardwood floor. How right it is
to be on my knees gathering these pebbles

into my hand while my refrigerator
purrs like a cat to make things cold.

Sauna Prana

Darkness of a cedar-slatted
small room, sizzling stones
of summer, salty river
of my body, naked, palms
upturned—it feels good
here, noticing my breath, my
    thoughts as they go
where they go. Sweat
dewdrops my skin, naked
as a jaybird's screech
of wanting from the woods
outside. For dinner I want
sweet corn, yellow nuggets
swathed in silken
    thread. Then the door
       swings, sliver of light
cracks my solitude, a face
    framed in black
          hair falling
to shoulders, rounded
       hips, brambled
     patch of Eden. Thought
leaps to Mexico—rosy green
    streaks of dawn. Cathedral
chimes, call to prayer. Nerve,
breath, tongue. *Hi, how are you?*
    Doin' well, thanks.
Desire, a white bird, egret
or trumpet swan, snow white
on naked wind—I watch it soar
to the horizon, never out of sight.

How Many Faces Do You Have?

I like to be touched, says Alicia, words
splashing against me like rain on tulips.
Spring thirst & the early bird catches

words fresh from her mouth. *The art
of living*, she says, *means take the gift
of yourself seriously.* It's good to hold

you, I say to her skin that holds sunlight
& warms me until we're empty & sleep
fills us & we don't exist. Love arrives

in shiny raindrops, she dreams, each of us,
as if thought by Magritte, holding an
unremarkable black umbrella. The hotel

bellman, face of wrinkled bronze beneath
the brim of a brown bowler, crimson
jacket, buttons polished gold. *What do you like*

most about yourself? he asks, eyes flaming
blue. Each moment bleeds into the next soldier
home from war, beribboned, handsome

with sadness. Is this my father? Poems
like money hidden in shoes, many shoes
in the room. Alicia's not here. The bellman,

his eyes—how can I answer? *I treat people
well*, he says & turns away. I drop tender green
in his brass spittoon, open mouthed, a rictus,

a scream. *I like to be touched*, says Alicia.
To be free as a river means want nothing
outside yourself. The art of living

is sun-sparkled dew on tulips. *How
many faces do you have?* In a startling
moment, a woman once asked me this, eyes

deadbolted with mine. She flashed ten of her
most beautiful & terrifying faces. Seconds
passed. Then she asked, *How many more?*

Fou d'Asie, Montreal

Blame the crazy Asian food.
Joie de vivre dans la nuit. Blame
Kevin, Julianne, Nelleke & me.
We savor foreign tongues—
gezellig, Flemish for bubbly
good time, and feast on conger
eel with avocado wrapped
in seaweed, speckled with red roe
from a fish that flies. Skin-like
scrapings of ginger flicker
in the mouth like tiny flames.
Taste buds sing *amour.*
      Across the street in pulsing neon,
Danseuses Nues, Spectacles Erotique,
lust lights the night. Convivial
as D'Artagnan & the musketeers,
we laugh at rituals of loneliness
& talk of ten-thousand stones
aligned like perfect teeth
in the *Cimetiére Mont-Royal.*
      Chablis & a guitar's wordless
sorrow weave with the lift & pause
of Kevin's voice. He was in love.
She wasn't. *C'est la vie.* At first light
he left & became an artist. Julianne
smiles. Her lips, glossed scarlet, float
disembodied & enormous in icy
air above a winter forest—as in
the painting by Man Ray. She knows
Kevin's story is mine. Nelleke.
Sound of her name. Can you feel it?
Unbearably tender pressure
of what I don't know how to say.
Nelleke. They've left the table, all
but me, gone to get their coats & pay.
Someone had to write this poem.

I Want You

in your pink underwear
        that makes me think
                of jelly beans, want you

as if you were an inscrutable
        message within me. Want to chew

& swallow mouthfuls
        of you. And still want you, Monday,
                Tuesday in the old garage

where it's cool & smells like oil
        & my father's tools on the wall

are there to be used like I want to be
        used by you, to wear each other

inside out like work shirts worn
    past threadbare. My hand, how it wants
      to be a sail that can lift

& make you fly, as if you were milkweed
        that bursts into seeds
                lighting the blackness

around us. And the aftersmell—
        morning fog, sweetfern
                flaked with pepper.

Love Me Like the First Word

hello, that rises from loneliness
& what the hell & artificial
flowers in cheap hotels become fragrant
& fragile & you know it won't last

but the country radio plays
slide ukulele blues & the DJ
says Maui & a wave
lifts us with long green fingers

until there's a pool
of underwear & you love me
generously as Brahms, that B-flat
murmur of the cello opening
a door to blue-blazed April

sky of the mind & we forget
all warning of storm, caught
in our experiment like amoebas
in a drop of pondwater
& a biologist somewhere

watching says Holy Shit
as boundaries dissolve & I become
a tadpole, sprout legs, climb
onto a lilypad, croak

to the Rose Moon of summer, round
& white enough to swallow me
as the egg swallows one anointed
sperm & the rest, millions of them,

die trying, while cellphones ring
all over the planet & spy satellites
fall from orbit & olive trees in Madagascar
blanch at our beautiful shamelessness

as you love me like poverty
the mother of crime, death
the mother of beauty, Zappa
the mother of invention

until I'm motherless
as Seth on Craig Street
with his plastic cup where my quarter
lands with a clink & he says God
Bless & I feel lucky to have breath
& change in my pocket

as you love me majestically spread-winged
as a condor on a thermal updraft in the Andes—
that easy, floating, to stay right there

until I cry
& every word
means tenderness, every gesture
kindness & I forgive my parents
& even the rattle of the air conditioner is joyful noise
like old bones getting ready to dance.

Buenos Aires

I'm not the *I love you* that signs off a phone call
as if filling out a form, she says. I'm the kiss

that says OK, here's a wet one for you on the lips—
now leave me alone cause it's the frayed end

of the day & your breath of nerves & steel
coffee reminds me how tired I am, seeing

you come through my door in that well
meaning, innocuous way, when what I want

is to be chopped & sizzled, defenses obliterated
like Vesuvius obliterated the merchants

& whores, mothers & lovers of Pompeii.
All in a day's work. Like kitchen roaches

in nuclear winter, you & I survive. We
go on. The inane Q & A proceeds. Please

give me a toothache. A new appliance. A layer
of fresh snow. A minute to compose myself.

This flash fire stoked by low wind downslope
from the mountain has withered to embers

& you keep trying to be some kind of poem
about daffodils while the sky roars with dandelion

laughter, thousands of tiny parachutes in slow
descent beginning to begin all over again.

Patches

With your Singer machine
           you stitched & grafted
patches to the knees
       of my favorite jeans.
And as I step into them,
    one leg after the other sliding

into that darkness of worn
       denim, I think of cone snails
& how from festively
         patterned shells they strike
with paralyzing venom, a fact
         unrelated to the way

I see you now, one of Munch's
         dangerous maidens
sunning in the shallows
       of a brook, naked,
legs spread, half wicked
      smile playfully inviting

me to dive
    headlong like Tarzan
into the lagoon. Jungle birds cry out
      as shadowy waters
part & now I'm Jane, dazzled
         beyond boarding school

to silence, gasping
  for air. Beauty makes sex
sex, said Anne
  Carson, thinking of Keats,
who coughed up
   blood on his pillow

& died, said his friends,
   of too much love
for Fanny Brawne. How
  does affection turn
to pleasure in power
   over another? Side-by-side

on top of the sheets, hands
   touching, no words,
not even moving,
  just breathing, we let
the night come down
   & settle upon us
like an enormous
  dark-winged bird.

Warning Label

She should have come
with a warning label, a tattoo
in purple script would do.
        It could say Handle with care.
It could say Powder me with Johnson's
                Baby Powder up
& down the hillsides of my perfectly
contoured gluteus max you will want
to hold & lift toward you in shuddering
communion as needed & for best
results nightly. It could say Generously
apply your desire to become
part of me intravenously
as transfused blood. It would warn
Be prepared (oh Boy Scouts of love)
for the expiration date of my affection.
It will not be a dream, though it feels like
the ground is withdrawn beneath
you, when the pretty girl inside my face
is replaced by a strange woman, inert
as a paring knife that peels
                your tenderness in strips.

Archibald Katydid

This is a poem for August evenings
with Archibald, the alpha katydid
of our backwoods grove
of sturdy oaks. As the sky reddens
he awakens & begins to crank
his ratchety hurdy-gurdy, incessantly
scratchy music for Jeni & me. To be
in dissonance happily as we feast
on avocado—leathery-skinned, pale
fruit called by Aztecs *ahuacătl*,
testicle, for its seed. And mangos, mouth-juicy
sweet, sunny yellow—two
of summer's perfect things. On this
we agree. Archibald play on. Then my sweetheart
remembers—robo-call from Giant Eagle, not the great
beaked warrior, but our friendly supermarket
named for a flying predator who doesn't eat fruit
or vegetables. The mangos may harbor
salmonella, not the heart-throb Italian
actor. *Salmonella*, troublesome
bacterium, yet another way for us
to die. Archibald, undaunted, rubs the edge
of one wing over the pegged ridge of the other,
rasping his lustful mambo serenade. *Not to worry*

is the least we do for our kids, says Jeni. She lifts
a glass of her favorite Roussanne. Tattletale
Archibald rattles on: *Katy did! She did!*
Something *Bad.* As in *Good. It's the brain's*
running backstory, says Jeni. *Shoulda. Shoulda*
listened to Mom. But what fun not to, say the crickets
tinkling their marimbas in the trees, descant to Casals
on the stereo, scratching his bow across four strings
tuned in perfect fifths, Bach's Suites. Blackness
overhead—one star, a pinprick opening
to the bright world outside this bag we're in,
ripening in darkness like an avocado.

One Day as Jeni Went On

about me, the amber stones
of her eyes flashed & I thought of IEDs
& chided myself—Defuse yourself
buddy, I muttered & breathed in
the lavender scent of soap that rubs
her skin pink. Years ago, gray pre-dawn
winter in the Allegheny Forest, a great horned
owl swept from a low branch, its beak
a pickaxe. Huge, yellow-irised eyes
assessed & passed me by. Beauty
can shake you down
to your boots like that. Silver earrings
bounced light from the side
of Jeni's face. I want to touch
her cheek, but not right now
I said to myself as it struck me
that her attractions don't exist
outside the splendor of Cleopatra—
the moment she coaxed the asp
to strike her breast, beauty
of that Go fuck yourself, Rome,
refusal. Icy inner mind
to resist. Vengeance, an engine
purring in every darkness or cemetery
mist. I heard a melody like rain
touching a piano, a tune almost
not a tune, the sound of her shuffling away
in fleecy slippers too big for her small feet.

Undercover

Undulant in cotton jammies, soft
pink. Hebraic raven
hair unfurled, fleecy
slippered, she shuffles into the room
where many nights our lives overlap
in space. This place needs more
than a scrape & paint job, she says, more
than to be replastered. Our revels have
unraveled, she says. Chicken Little
says The sky is falling. And it is—
98.7 percent of me that's chimpanzee, blasted
with hurt. While the robust gorilla man
of me dons his mask of a thousand
romances. Oh Captain, my Captain
Kangaroo, why doesn't she draw
from the voluminous pocket of her blazer
a voluptuous yellow-green big bunch
of bananas & say Ooooo? To uproot
ourselves as if plucking from its stem a grape
at fullest blush—gently now, the cold
war is endless & has no heroes. One
night in August, a slow-moving
meteor ripped a white slash
across the sky. Right before our eyes
       closed. Did we really see that?

He Dreams a Woman Who's a Ship

after "The Ship," Dalí, 1942-43

I am a ship.
I am the body of a woman.
My breasts scud the waves
         that roll across me like briny
lips. My hips are green water
     & undertow. I wear a necklace
of teeth. The moon talks
only to me. Many nights drawn
     to sea-worn men, I take
them with me, tumbling
         among cuttlefish, nacre
& mollusk. In my hold, I show them
priceless cargo—charred bones
         of war, eyelids
             peeled from eyes seared
     from seeing, tongues
     of nothing to say. By stars
I navigate fathomless oceans
         to find harbor, my mother's
wounded beauty. To feel
     the torn away fish-hooks, spasms
         of that voyage into light
     when my body
was hers. Only a woman
             can do this, tangle
     of rigging, jangled
wire. Sea-wind gusts my seaweed
hair. Flotsam, screaming gull, scent
of humus. I am the windflower, anemone.
A new world. The awful step forward.

The Trouble With Love

The trouble with love,
        says a friend of mine,
is you give it an inch
       it takes you dancing,
takes you to lunch
    & the cleaners, takes you
where your mother said
       Don't go. And your father
went & came home
        begging forgiveness.

The trouble with love
       is ice cracks, Earth
howls when love arrives
      like a crocus in spring
if it could cry with joy
        as it heaves toward light.
Open the windows. Love
     is the best drug there is.

The trouble with love
       is hit the road Jack.
You're an empty sack.
        To be alive is to lose
the world like Bonaparte,
     alone on that high shelf
of the fire escape
       where you look down
at your feet. And think

the trouble with love
      is a wild white flag, yearling
doe in a distant snowfield,
    flashing, gone, bloodhound
sniffing a scorched trail
        into the tangled heartland
where there is no trail, blue
         hole in a cold blue sky.
Under a flat stone, you find
   a note you once wrote to yourself.
It says, The trouble with love.

The Way Your Fingers

curl around the belly
of a cello, carved maple
burnished to glow, almost alive
as you lift & place it
like precious pearl
into the shell
of its case, because music
has ended & the spine
loosens as nerves gather waves
from the air, after-music
awakened in the hollow of the bones

the way words of a poem
wait their turn, shuffling down corridors
until you least expect a door
to open, mouth to move
& say Leaves of the sweetgum tree
are yellow stars
fallen into your hand, as if the sky
could shatter in small pieces, each
torn fragment pungent
as bread in the morning, when you & I
are gloriously alone, time
having strangely failed
to move us, blanket rumpled, sheet
twisted between us

the way your hand like a boat
on dark water rowed
across the distance that night
you touched my wrist, how
it became this moment: sun
lifting from blackness
to slant through the blinds
& brighten your hair
on the pillow beside me. Everything
is here, right here.

River Under Ice

April morning. Light
leaps through a window.
      What happens
in the mind's eye
    happens—you & I
      specks of dust
jitterbugging in a sunbeam
          toward each other.

*

We're seeds a blackbird
       dropped in a meadow.
To soak in the sun & rain
    of each other, to flower
untamed, to heal a wound
      that never closes.

The river is moving under the ice.

*

We'll remember July, hillside
by the old school, swath
    of tailfeathers fallen
from a small brown bird
      I held in my hand
   for you to see it breathing.

Sparks in the Air

Some afternoons I'd climb
the hill, up from Elk Creek
to the dirt & gravel alley
behind Uncle Bill's garage.
I'd tuck a stem of meadowgrass
between my teeth, bite down
& get the taste of it, reach
the hilltop soon enough
& look back to the other side
of town. I'd climb the big sugar
maple, sit cradled in the upward
straining of its arms & fat hands
waving as wild geese flew
overhead. Where's their home?
I'd wonder as cool fingers of air
brushed my skin. I'd watch
a slow parade of clouds become
stallions, a giant squid from Jules
Verne or the prow of a Viking ship
looming out of fogbank toward
adventure with young Prince
Valiant of the Sunday
comics at the helm. Now

    from a bluff above
the sea, I watch the sun
run out of sky, staining the horizon
watermelon red. A freighter groans
toward harbor. Somewhere
out there a hemlock-masted schooner
with all hands went down. Fragrance
of a pine. Old Spice
& turpentine. Do you love
how seagulls hover? That reedy
screech of raw desire mixed
with sorrow. Stars come out

to string the sky with beasts
& heroes. Let's build a fire, you
& I, right here—light a blaze
of sparks & watch it swirl upward
in the moonlight. Make a wish. Night's
a dancehall & it's a polka, sweetheart.
Let's kick our heels like we mean it
& twirl for happiness that's real.

CPSIA information can be obtained
at www.ICGtesting.com
Printed in the USA
LVOW10s0518090517

533760LV00001B/12/P